THE UNITED STATES
NAVY

by Tracy Vonder Brink

W0006496

PEBBLE
a capstone imprint

Pebble Explore is published by Pebble, an imprint of Capstone.
1710 Roe Crest Drive, North Mankato, Minnesota 56003
www.capstonepub.com

Library of Congress Cataloging-in-Publication Data
Names: Vonder Brink, Tracy, author.
Title: The United States Navy / by Tracy Vonder Brink.
Description: North Mankato, Minnesota : Pebble, An Imprint of
Capstone, [2021] | Series: All about branches of the U.S. military |
Includes bibliographical references and index. | Audience: Ages 6-8 |
Audience: Grades 2-3 | Summary: "The U.S. Navy traces its roots back to
the American Revolutionary War. Then, its small fleet was outnumbered.
Today, it is the largest navy in the world. Learn about the roles of
sailors and their training, and get an inside look at the different
types of ships, aircraft, equipment, and weapons the U.S. Navy uses to
complete missions around the world"-- Provided by publisher.
Identifiers: LCCN 2020026183 (print) | LCCN 2020026184 (ebook) | ISBN
9781977131768 (library binding) | ISBN 9781977155092 (pdf)
Subjects: LCSH: United States. Navy--Juvenile literature.
Classification: LCC VA58.4 .V66 2021 (print) | LCC VA58.4 (ebook) | DDC
359.00973--dc23
LC record available at https://lccn.loc.gov/2020026183
LC ebook record available at https://lccn.loc.gov/2020026184

Image Credits
U.S. Navy photo: 28, U.S. Navy photo by Burrell Parmer, 6, Chief Boatswain's Mate Nelson Doromal Jr, 13 (Bottom), Chris Oxley, 20, Lt. Alex Cornell du Houx, 25, Mass Communication Specialist 1st Class Amanda S. Kitchner, 7, Mass Communication Specialist 1st Class Carmichael Yepez, 11 (Bottom), Mass Communication Specialist 1st Class Peter Lewis, 24, Mass Communication Specialist 1st Class Ryan U. Kledzik, 17, Mass Communication Specialist 2nd Class Christian Senyk, 19 (Top), Mass Communication Specialist 2nd Class Jason Isaacs, 4, Mass Communication Specialist 2nd Class Kelsey L. Adams, 29, Mass Communication Specialist 2nd Class Kyle Carlstrom, 15, Mass Communication Specialist 2nd Class Spencer Fling, 5, Mass Communication Specialist 2nd Class Tamara Vaughn, 8, Mass Communication Specialist 2nd Class Thomas Gooley, 14, 21, Mass Communication Specialist 2nd Class Tony D. Curtis, 27 (Top), Mass Communication Specialist 3rd Class Benjamin Waddell, 23, Mass Communication Specialist 3rd Class Erick A. Parsons, Cover, Mass Communication Specialist 3rd Class Lenny LaCrosse, 13 (Top), Mass Communication Specialist 3rd Class Michele Fink, 27 (Bottom), Mass Communication Specialist 3rd Class Samuel Gruss, 19 (Bottom), Mass Communication Specialist 3rd Class Tyler N. Thompson, 16, Mass Communication Specialist Seaman Alexander Williams, 22, Mass Communication Specialist Seaman Carla Ocampo, 11 (Top), Mass Communication Specialist William C. Andrews, 9

Design Elements
Capstone; Shutterstock: CRVL, Zerbor

Editorial Credits
Editor: Carrie Sheely; Designer: Kayla Rossow; Media Researcher: Jo Miller; Production Specialist: Laura Manthe

All internet sites appearing in back matter were available and accurate when this book was sent to press.

Printed in the United States   4828

Table of Contents

Words in **bold** are in the glossary.

WHAT IS THE NAVY?

A Navy destroyer travels on the sea. An enemy ship fires at it. Boom! The Navy ship fires back.

The United States Navy is a branch of the U.S. **military**. It formed more than 200 years ago. The Navy fights at sea. It has more than 400,000 members. They are called sailors.

Sailors can be on active duty or in the Reserve. Active-duty sailors serve full-time. Sailors in the Reserve work part-time. They become active duty when they are needed.

JOINING THE NAVY

Men and women can join the Navy.
They must be between 17 and 39
years old. U.S. **citizens** can join. Some
noncitizens who live lawfully in the
United States can also join. All must
be healthy and fit.

After joining, new sailors go to basic training. It takes seven weeks. The new sailors exercise. They swim. They learn to use **weapons**. They learn to work together.

Each sailor gets a job after training. Some help sail ships. Others fix boats or fire guns on boats. Some become rescue swimmers. Others are divers. Some are doctors or nurses. There are more than 90 kinds of jobs.

Active-duty sailors work on a base. There are more than 40 Navy bases in the United States. A base is like a town for sailors. The sailors live on or near the base. Their families can live with them.

Sometimes sailors are **deployed**. They must leave their homes. The Navy might be needed to fight or protect an area at sea. Ships usually deploy once every 18 to 24 months. Sailors can be gone for up to nine months. The sailors return when they are done.

11

NAVY UNIFORMS AND GEAR

Sailors wear different uniforms. Sailors often wear Navy Working Uniforms on shore. Navy SEALs wear them in battle. The **camouflage** of the uniforms makes it hard for enemies to see the fighters. Dress uniforms are for parades and special events.

Navy Working Uniforms

dress uniforms

The Navy has planes. Some sailors are pilots. They wear flight suits. These suits keep pilots comfortable when they fly.

Some sailors fix ships and planes.
It can be dirty work. The Navy doesn't
want sailors to look dirty. Those
who work these jobs wear dark blue
coveralls.

Navy divers wear wet suits. The suits keep them warm. They also wear scuba gear with an air tank. It gives them air to breathe underwater. Masks keep water out of the eyes.

Rescue swimmers wear masks with **snorkels**. Snorkel tubes can poke out above the water. Swimmers can breathe through them when near the water's surface. Rescue swimmers also wear life jackets. They can fill the jackets with air if they need to float.

NAVY VEHICLES AND MACHINES

The Navy has many ships and boats. Some are for fighting battles. Others are for carrying people and gear. Some carry planes.

Destroyers are powerful attack ships. Some destroyers can carry a crew of more than 300 sailors. They can fire more than 90 **missiles**. The missiles hit **targets** on land and at sea.

destroyer

Submarines are boats that travel under the water. They can dive deeper than 800 feet (244 meters). They fire at enemy ships from below. They also attack enemy submarines. Fast attack submarines can fire missiles through the air. They carry crews of more than 100.

The SSBN "boomer" is one kind of submarine. It is only used to attack land targets. It sneaks underwater close to enemy land. Then it fires powerful missiles.

A Navy aircraft carrier is like an airport on the water. Planes take off from and land on it. It has a crew of more than 3,000 sailors. It can carry more than 60 planes.

Many aircraft carriers have F/A-18s. These fast planes can fly more than 1,000 miles (1,069 kilometers) per hour. They can attack enemy planes or ground targets.

Sometimes the Navy needs to carry sailors and supplies where the water isn't deep. The Riverine Command Boat (RCB) is a little longer than a school bus. It can travel on rivers. It can also go from the sea to the shore. The RCB has machine guns and other weapons.

Some Navy vehicles go where it's too deep for people to dive. The CURV-21 can go 20,000 feet (6,096 m) deep. Sailors on a ship guide it by **remote control**. It finds boats and other machines that have sunk.

LIFE IN THE NAVY

Deployed sailors live on their ships at sea. They eat, sleep, and work there. They each have a locker to store their gear. To save space, they have bunk beds. During the day, they do their jobs. They also clean the ships. Sailors have some free time too.

Some deployed sailors live on submarines. Submarines don't have much room inside. Sailors take turns sleeping in bunk beds.

Sailors stay in the Navy between four and eight years. Some join again. They make the Navy their **career**.

Sailors go to rescue a boat crew.

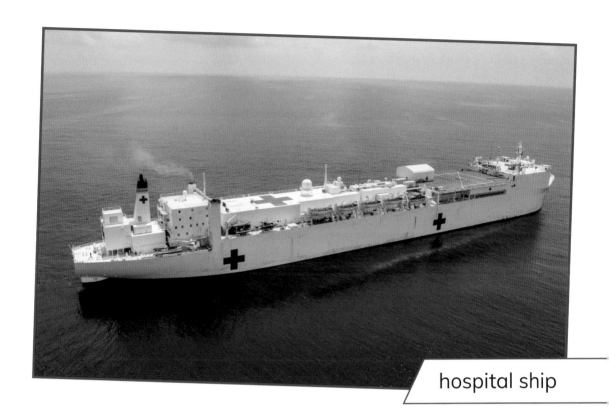

hospital ship

Navy sailors are always ready to help. They fight enemies. They rescue people in trouble at sea. They bring supplies to thosc in need. Sailors on hospital ships help people who are sick or hurt. The brave sailors of the U.S. Navy work hard to protect the country every day.

GLOSSARY

camouflage (KA-muh-flahzh)—patterns and colors designed to make military uniforms, gear, and weapons blend in with a given natural setting

career (kuh-REER)—the type of work a person does, usually over many years

citizen (SI-tuh-zuhn)—a member of a country or state who has the right to live there

deploy (di-PLOY)—to move troops into position for military action

military (MIL-uh-ter-ee)—the armed forces of a country

missile (MISS-uhl)—a weapon that is shot through the air

remote control (ri-MOHT kuhn-TROHL)—a device used to control machines from a distance

snorkel (SNOR-kul)—a tube used to let a person breathe underwater

target (TAR-git)—an object at which to aim or shoot

weapon (WEP-uhn)—something used for fighting

READ MORE

Marx, Mandy R. *Amazing U.S. Navy Facts*. North Mankato, MN: Capstone Press, 2017.

Miller, Nancy. *My Mom Is in the Navy*. New York: PowerKids Press, 2016.

Reed, Jennifer. *The U.S. Navy*. North Mankato, MN: Capstone Press, 2018.

INTERNET SITES

Ducksters: U.S. Government: United States Armed Forces
www.ducksters.com/history/us_government/united_states_armed_forces.php

Kiddle: United States Navy Facts for Kids
kids.kiddle.co/United_States_Navy

Science Kids: Submarine Facts for Kids
www.sciencekids.co.nz/sciencefacts/vehicles/submarines.html

INDEX